With Best Wishes

With best wishes

Cherrie Almond

With Best Wishes

A selection of poems on life itself

By

Cherrie Almond

with additional historical material
by Geoff Pushman

and sketches by Fleur Fenner

SCRIPT TECHNOLOGY PUBLICATIONS

2006

First published by Val Randall
December 1971
Reprinted January 1974

Republished by
Script Technology Publications
stpubs@btinternet.com

Poems © 1971-2006 Cherry Almond
Historical material © 1948-53 Geoff Pushman
Sketches © 2006 Fleur Fenner

Material from "Geoff's Banstead"
by kind permission of Mark Newell

A catalogue record for this book is available
from the British Library

ISBN 0-9554251-0-7   (10 digit)
ISBN 978-0-9554251-0-3   (13 digit)

Printed by the Print Solutions Partnership,
88 Sandy Lane South, Wallington, Surrey SM6 9RQ
Tel: 020 8404 3922 email: print@pspartnership.co.uk

Contents

Foreword. v
Foreword to first edition (December 1971) vii
DELUSION. 2
LIVING ALONE. 4
THE SAILOR'S WIFE. 6
CRIPPLESPATH 8
AUTUMN 10
TO THE TREE THAT GUARDS THE COTTAGE 12
THE MOON 14
THE OAK 16
LOST HOPE. 18
THE RETREAT GARDEN 20
BY THE BLUE LAKE SWITZERLAND. 22
DREAM OF YOUTH. 24
BANSTEAD IN 1920. 25
OLD BANSTEAD 27
NONSENSE RHYMES. 28
SAN SALVATORE 30
SEPTEMBER. 32
PAGHAM 34
THE GATE 36
WRITTEN FOR THE HARRASSED LANDLADY
AT THE CARFAX. 38
RESIGNATION. 40
A MEMORY 42
AUTUMN AGAIN 44
CONCLUSION 46
Cherrie's Banstead. 47
How Cherrie Almond came to Banstead 48
The Ferndale Concert Party. 52
Willie Nash 61
The Banstead War Memorial 64

Banstead Woods (from an old engraving)

FOREWORD

Looking over some old cards and photographs for the second volume of the History of Banstead I came across a greeting card with an engraving of Banstead Wood. In addition to the greeting inside the card this captivating stanza from a poem was also included:

> *'Twas unspoiled English beauty with hedgerows all along,*
> *Fringed thick with beech and chestnut, alive with wild birdsong;*
> *And many a gallant homestead lay in its garden fair,*
> *Like jewels in their setting, with blossoms often rare.*

The stanza came from the book entitled "The Poems of Cherrie Almond" by Cherrie Almond.

"Who was Cherrie Almond?", Fortunately, someone had thoughtfully added in pencil: "Geoff Pushman's Mother". I had known Geoff but was unaware that his mother had married a Mr. Almond after the death of her first husband, Mr. Pushman. So, instead of being Mrs. Cherrie Pushman she became Mrs. Cherrie Almond!

Enticed by the stanza I wanted to read more of the poem and the others in the book. No problem, I thought, there must be a copy of the book of poems in the local library in Banstead - after all, Geoff and his mother were well known to all the locals in the area. Sadly, I was out of luck. No copy existed in the library, Surrey History Centre, the British Library or even on the internet. Even the secondhand booksellers I visited didn't have a copy or had even heard of the book. Local historians were equally not much help. Some had known Mrs. Almond and had seen one or two of her poems but not the entire book. I concluded that I was looking for a needle in a haystack!

All attempts to find the book seemed to come to nothing. In December 2004, my friend, Ronald Diack, managed to track down a copy of this rare book, which, as luck would have it, belonged to an acquaintance of his. To my great delight, I finally read the poem whose captivating lines had started the quest. The enticing stanza came from the poem "Banstead in 1920".

Having endured a long search for the book, I decided that it should be reprinted if only to ensure that the poems were made known to current and future generations. To this end, copies of this book will be deposited at the local library in Banstead, the Surrey History Centre and the British Library. This is a not-for-profit publication. All contributions for the book are passed on to the Children's Trust Charity (Tadworth).

In addition to the poems in the original book, I have included another poem, "Old Banstead", which appeared in the November 1951 issue of the Banstead Spotlight. Fleur Fenner has also been inspired to create a series of sketches to accompany the poems.

Thanks are due to Mark Newall for allowing extracts from his book "Geoff's Banstead" to be printed and for photographs of Cherrie, her son Geoff and the Ferndale Concert party. Also to Mrs. Shelagh Jones for the photograph of Willie Nash who worked in Cherrie's shop as a grocers assistant. He was killed at the age of 21 in 1918 during the First World War. He was very popular. When news of his death reached Banstead everyone in the shop and customers alike were grief stricken.

Cherrie Almond passed away in 1977 aged 96 and is buried in All Saints' churchyard, Banstead.

Ralph Maciejewski,
Banstead, September 2006

FOREWORD TO FIRST EDITION
(December 1971)

Born at Tottenham, London, in 1880, Cherrie Almond's eventful life has brought her in contact with many famous personalities, among them being John Drinkwater, John Masefield, Alfred Noyes and Sir John Aird. She is probably the only living person to have met Florence Nightingale.

After training and working as a teacher in North London, Mrs. Almond bought a small general store in Banstead, Surrey in 1912, where she stayed until 1931. She was a founder member of the Banstead Choral Society and also formed the Ferndale Concert Party for which she supplied most of the original scripts and material. In 1931 Mrs. Almond moved to Pagham Beach near Bognor, leaving the tobacconist's and confectioner's section of the shop to her son Geoff who carries on the business to this day. In 1938 a further move was made, this time to St. Lawrence in the Isle of Wight, beautiful environs ideally suited to one of such artistic temperament.

Cherrie Almond writes of Life itself: her verses are of real places, real emotions, real people. Even her comical "Wallypug" must surely bear some resemblance to certain people we have met.

This little volume is far more than an achievement —it is an inspiration and an encouragement to all of us, for it was published in its author's 91st year — a defiant gesture to an age which bemoans "too old at forty".

Today Mrs. Almond lives at Niton Glen, Isle of Wight, still independent, still dynamic, still even doing her own painting and decorating (in addition to superb water-colour pictures) and still, we hope, writing more verses which may one day constitute another volume of "The Poems of Cherrie Almond".

Val. Randall. 1971

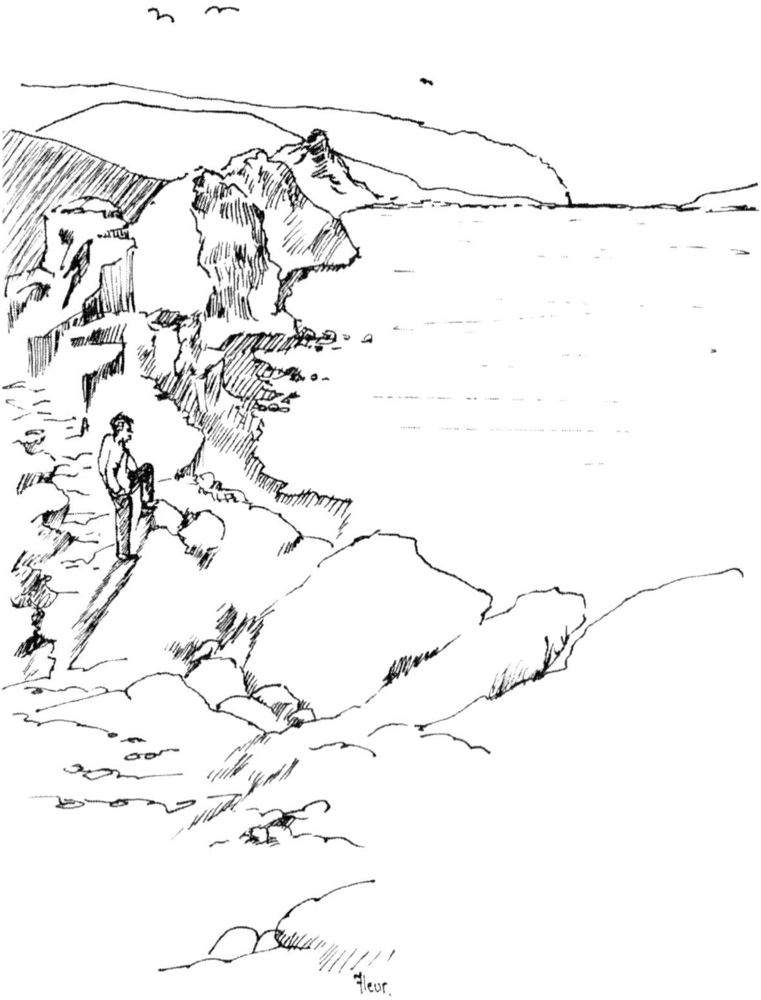
Fleur.

DELUSION

The sun shone bright on the glittering sea,
And the water like glass was as still as could be;
The sand, too, like gold lay an untrodden track
As the tide receded in smaller waves back.
The years fell away and I felt young and free
As I wandered along at the brink of the sea.

The sky grey and sullen with the rain splashing down,
The tall distant hills seemed to look down and frown
Whilst the breakers grey thundered and broke on the shore
Succeeded by others with ominous roar.
I shivered and drew my cloak closer still
As foreboding and sorrow my anxious mind fill.
Ah, youth is a fiction — I feel strangely old
As I totter up hill to my hearth dead and cold.

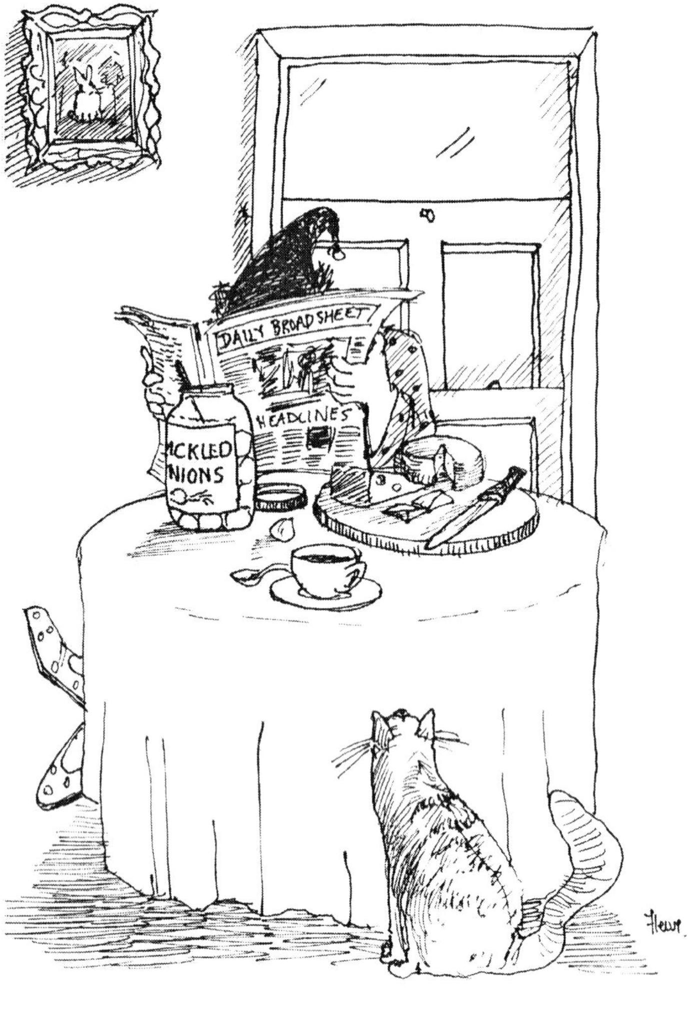
DAILY BROAD SHEET
HEADLINES
ICKLED
NIONS
Fleur

LIVING ALONE

You may get up early or late as you please;
If it's your fancy for breakfast eat pickled onions and cheese.
You may read the newspaper and learn all the news
And browse on conflicting political views.
No one to tell you do this or do that,
To turn out the bedrooms, or put out the cat.
You may lunch at mid-day, at one or at three —
A meat course, a sweet, or a wee pot of tea.
And when it grows dark and the fire's glowing red —
Some sewing, T.V., and then off to bed.

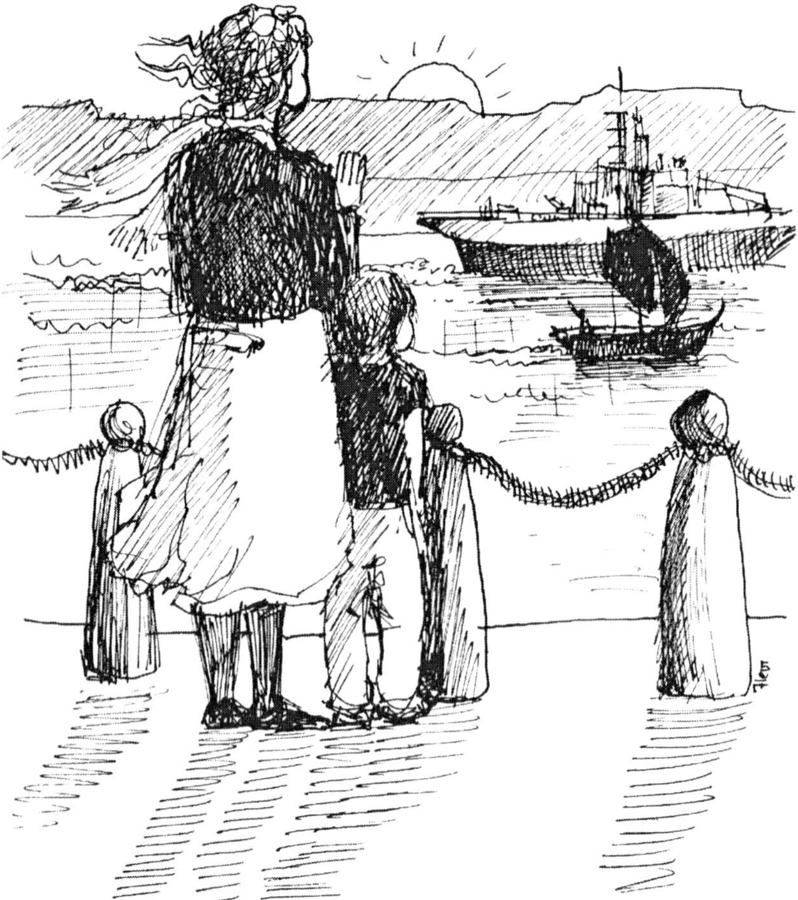

THE SAILOR'S WIFE

How wild was the night — the inky sky
Seemed to wrap itself round us — you and I,
And cut us off from all mortal ken,
And people the world with ghosts of men.

Though in terror dire of that inky black
I still would wish that dear moment back
That night before you went out to sea
When you bade adieu to the child and to me.

The ship set sail at the dawn of day,
And I stood depressed on the old stone quay.
The wind in a fury tore at my skirt,
But to fish in the sea is a strong man's work.

I watched your grey sail growing less and less,
And I prayed the good Lord your efforts to bless;
And I turned my unwilling feet away
To the mundane tasks of an anxious day.

I thought of the talk of the men on the shore
That your craft would ne'er see a winter more,
That its poor old hulk was a leaky sieve:
In a storm 'twould not have a chance to live.

I knew that the season was hard for you lad,
That the fish were shy and the trawl was bad,
But you laughed as you said that a timorous wife
Was surely the plague of a sailor's life.

The sun set soon in a sea of red,
The child slept restless in cradle bed,
The tramp of feet seemed to halt at my door:
It shook, and they whispered -those men from the shore.

The sun went down in a sea of red,
They tell me my man is drowned and dead.
The sky shows itself as an ocean of gold,
But the light of my life has gone out, and I'm cold.

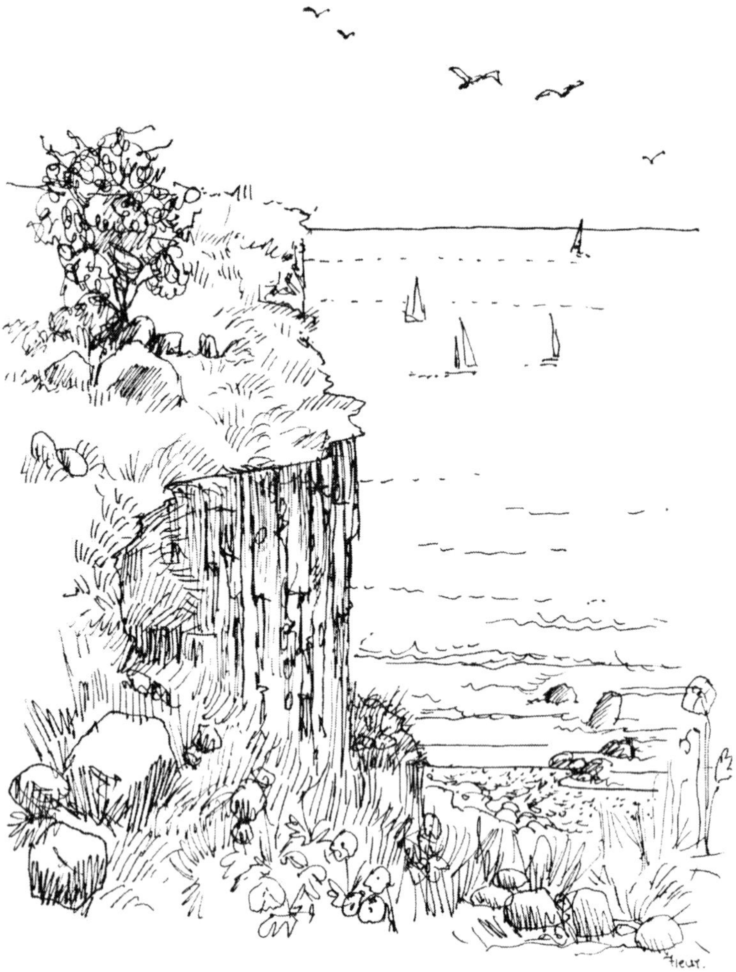
Fleur.

CRIPPLESPATH

The rugged cliff, so bold and free,
Stands sentinel to guard the sea,
And on its gnarled and rugged face
The lavish verdure grows apace.
The fairy glimpses in between
Of sea and cot —through leafy screen
And far away on azure blue
White sails of ships are passing too.
The languid breeze scarce seems to fill
The canvas sail that lies so still,
And I above, perched on a stone,
Feel like a queen upon her throne
With chaffinch for her minstrel sweet
Singing in woodland at her feet.

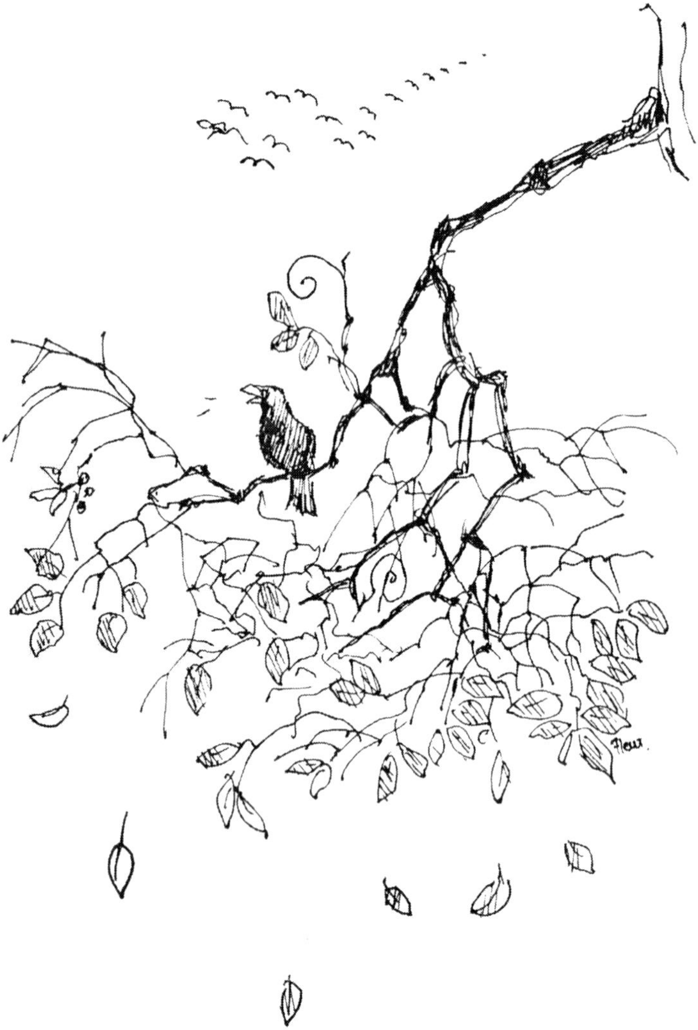

AUTUMN

The scent of a belated rose,
The crunching leaves a carpet brown,
The earthy smell of trodden ground,
The year that's drawing to a close.

The season of the yellow flowers,
The red and gold on every tree,
The tawny bracken on the lea,
The falling leaves, the shortening hours.

The Robin, singing Autumn's praise,
The wind soft sighing o'er the plain;
The haunting sadness comes again,
Elusive — through those wonder days.

The swollen stream that tears along
Past the tall grass all powdered white,
And birds that gather for their flight,
Bearing its load of leaves and song.

The thrush sings plaintively and slow,
The wispy clouds gather like sheep,
Giving the sun his chance to peep
On patches of loveliness below.

So Autumn with her magic wand
Makes of the earth a fairy land,
And with an artist's master hand
Paints tree and hill and ferny frond.

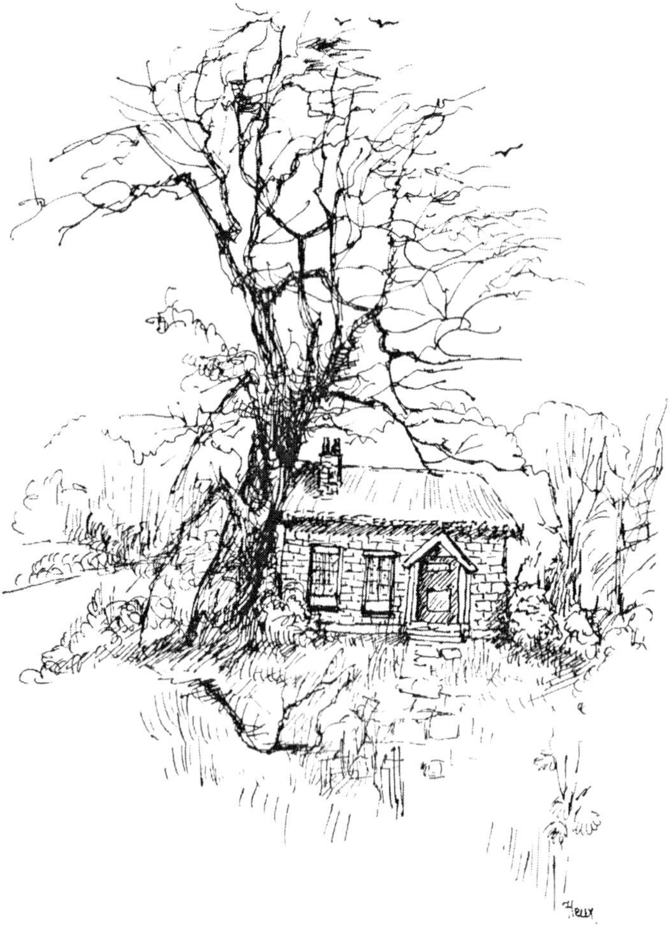
Helix

TO THE TREE THAT GUARDS
THE COTTAGE

Alas, poor tree, you stand alone on guard
Through biting cold and wintry weather hard
Outside the gate where once my true love dwelt
And in thy shadow Love's sweet presence felt;
The hovering lips that came to rest on mine,
Lifting me up to Heaven —once on a time.
And now, poor tree, you stand so tall and gaunt,
Branches all shorn — a nakedness you flaunt;
Dejected spectre of a glorious past,
You rear your head on high, a hideous mast.
Your graceful leaves and branches all are gone,
Your spacious limbs with ruthless weapons torn,
And my dear Love — my joy and my delight
Has gone away and I am left to fight
A giant Despair — a sword to pierce my heart.
Alas, I little dreamed he'd ever wish to part,
But now I wonder if he really cared for me,
Or ever did — or, like you, spoilt and lovely tree,
The living sap still flows — and still yet may
Burst forth in living green — for me one day.

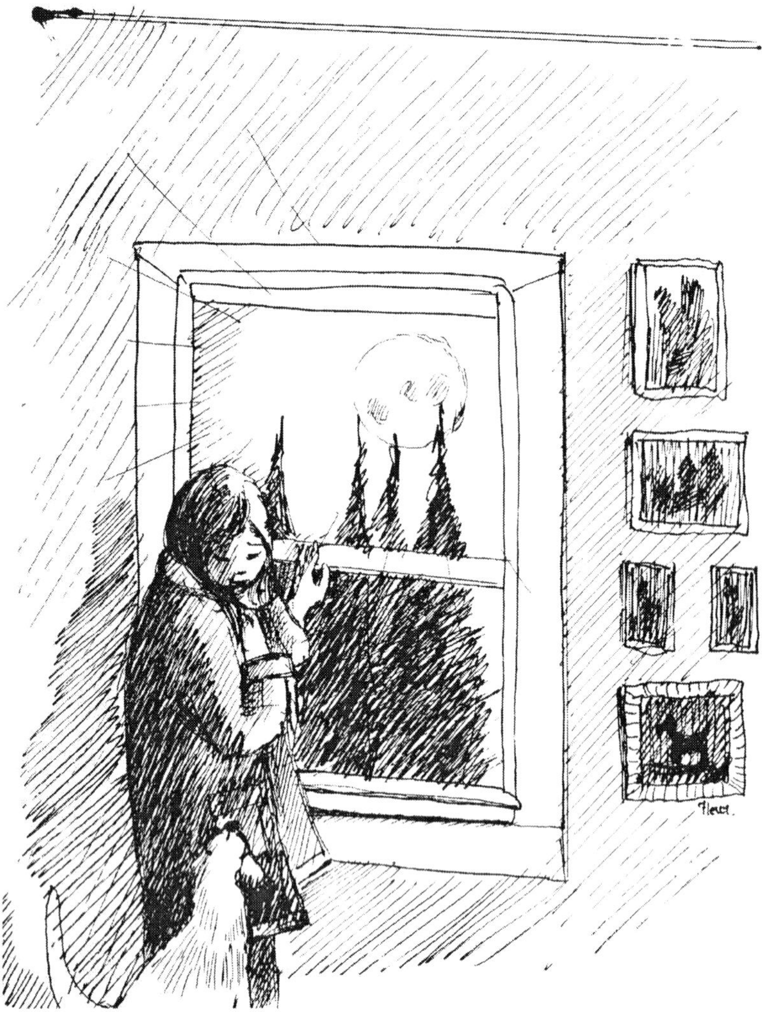
Fleur.

THE MOON

Dear moon — I loved you so when I was small,
But now I've grown I love you not at all.
You used to make the world so bright for me
That I could walk abroad at night and see
The world a fairyland, so silver white,
The fields, the trees, the flowers all bathed in light.

But now the moon a mocking spirit seems;
She shines on me in sleep and haunts my dreams.
Her light is harsh, her brilliance all revealing:
I want the inky blackness all concealing,
That I myself may creep away and hide
Now that the last faint gleam of hope has died.
For love's grown cold, and moon your mocking light
Brings back the things when life was a delight.
Oh, irony of light — there is no light.
I gaze into the night — I have no sight,
For I, alas, am blind — who yet can see,
Feeling alone remains — alas for me.

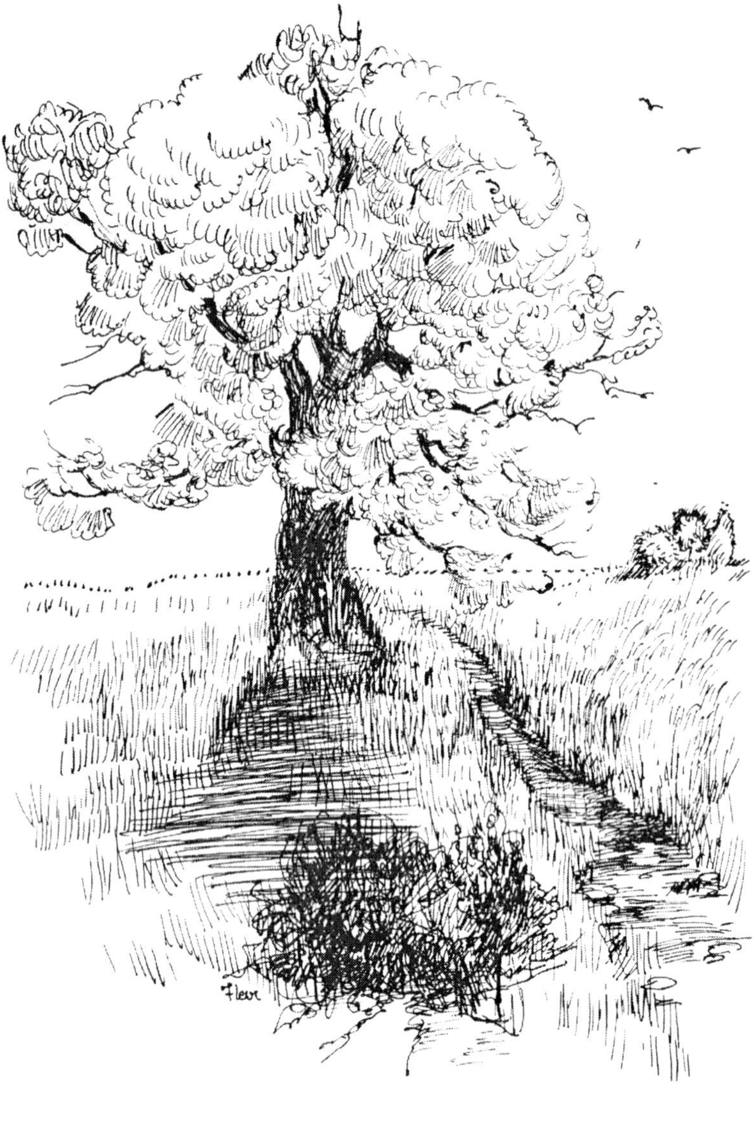
Fleur

THE OAK

Along the path my love is wont to tread,
With Autumn gold the leaves glow overhead;
When all was quiet I stole along the lane
And culled a branch to take me home again.
It was an oak I chose with gold aglow;
I pulled a branch that nearest was and low:
Each day it bent in greeting as you passed,
In summer's heat a grateful shade it cast,
And in the winter, bent by Arctic blast,
It bent upon you blessing as you passed.
I love that branch all gay with brown and gold
Culled from that oak tree sere and bent and old

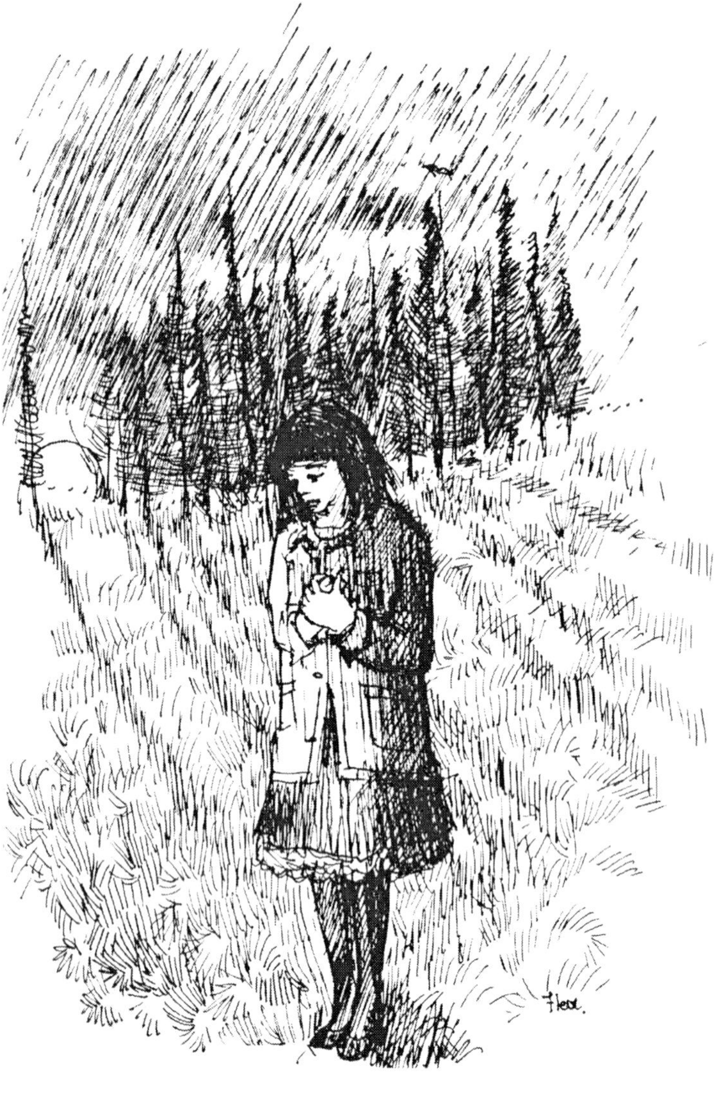

LOST HOPE

I have no lovely gift of song to give thee,
And day is dying quickly in the West;
The only gift, my darling, that is left me
I give thee — and thou knowest it is best.

For many years I've wandered sad and weary
With hopeful eyes for ever on a light,
And when things saddest grew and dreary
I kept that end for ever in my sight

The light was Love and Peace with you at ev'ning,
But time grows short and light is fading fast,
And I grow tired and weary of the waiting
And fear that Love is lost me at the last.

So though my heart breaks at the thought of parting,
It's for your good and so I'll say goodbye;
Loving you still above all hope and reason,
I'll walk alone in darkness till I die.

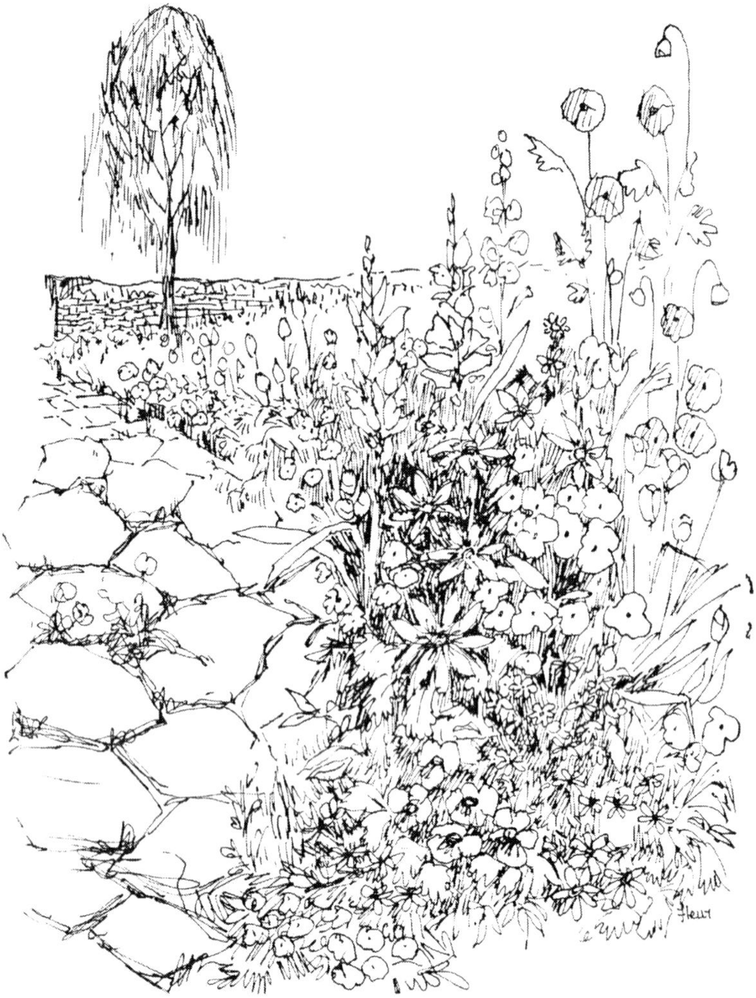
Fleur

THE RETREAT GARDEN

I came into a wilderness
Of brambles, furze and alder
Where birds and rats and rabbits too
All crept away to shelter.
I cleared the ground and dug away
The formless masses there,
And dug and delved and planted too
To make a garden fair.
I put me gilly flowers and ferns,
Anemones and daisy,
Columbines and crocus too,
And made a pavement crazy.
The tall twin alders stand on guard
One at each end so stately,
And now it's Spring I've seen some bloom
Primrose and crocus lately.
My head is full of plans to plant
And make it full of bloom,
For Spring has come, and so my pets
Will be a-blowing soon.

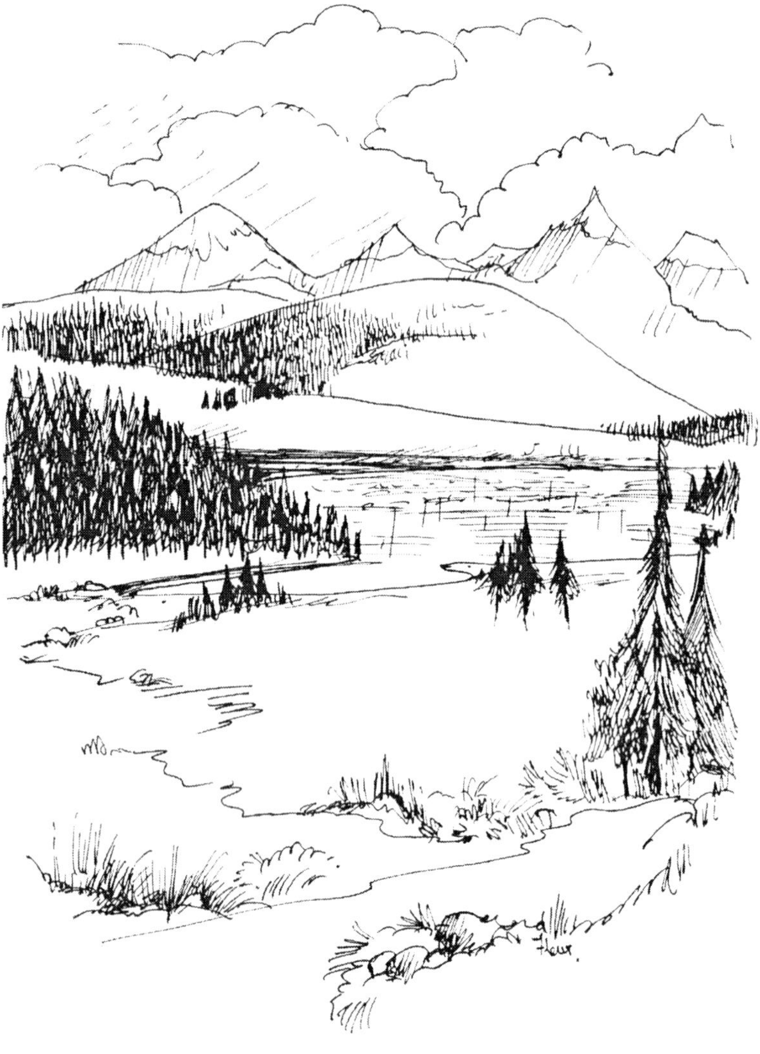

BY THE BLUE LAKE
SWITZERLAND

A jewel of blue in setting fair
Fanned gently by the Alpine air,
Hemmed in by mountains tall and grim,
Forests mysterious and dim.
Oh tell me whence this colour bright
That gives the soul such sweet delight.
Do those high peaks some secret hold
That we poor humans mayn't unfold?
Is this the gem upon their breast
Which lies so quietly there at rest
That all men come afar to see
This lake of blue and mystery?
Is it a piece of Heaven above
Set here to prove its Maker's love,
To tell us of that sapphire sea
Where our true home is yet to be question
Sit by this Blue Lake if you dare
And say its Maker is not there:
He shows Himself in flower and tree,
In mountain, lake and sunny sea;
He's seen in storm and floating cloud,
In lightning and thunder loud,
But the still small voice came soft to me
By that lake of blue and mystery.

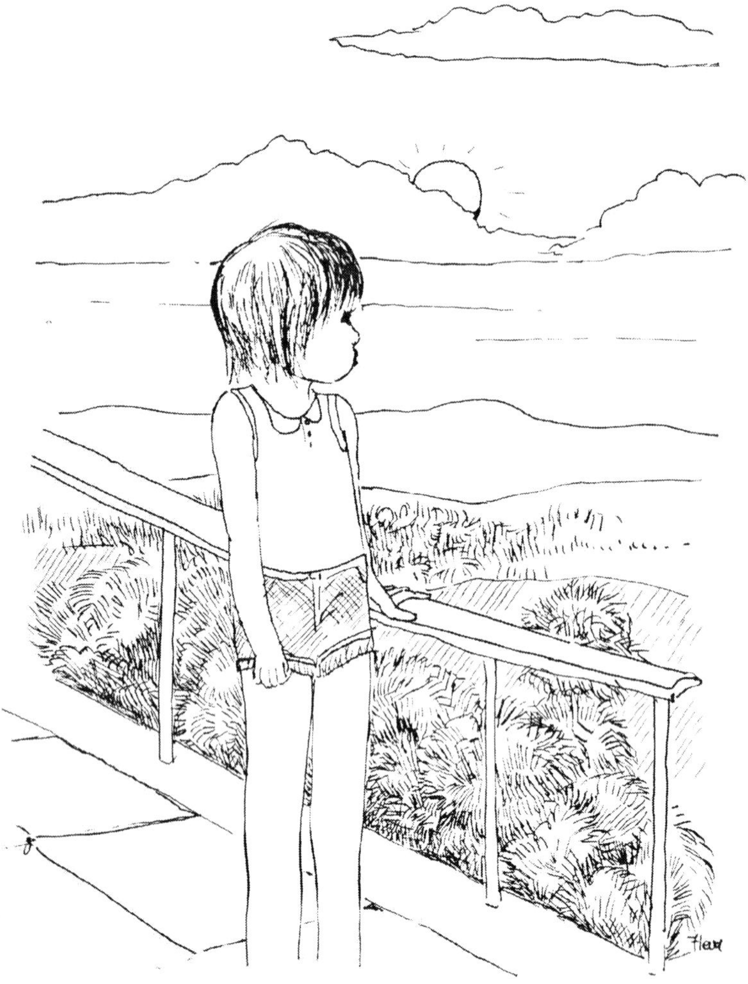

DREAM OF YOUTH

Gold in the sky! Gold in the sky!
Something will happen I'm sure bye and bye,
I'll think of you, love, and you'll think of me
Where e'er at this moment you happen to be.
I looked at the sky and I looked at the cloud,
And being alone I said it aloud —
All that is over me, all that's above,
Tell him I'm thinking with heart full of love,
Sending him messages, begging him come.
I'm waiting alone here, I'm waiting at home;
Tell him there's no one I want quite so much,
There's no one whose hand I'm so longing to touch.
He has power to break me and love p'raps to make me:
Ah, if he'd but come then how happy I'd be.

BANSTEAD IN 1920

When I first came to Banstead 'twas many years ago;
The lark sang in the heavens and roses were ablow.
I walked out in the country and breathed the sweet pure air,
And felt I could be happy in such a village fair.

'Twas unspoiled English beauty with hedgerows all along,
Fringed thick with beech and chestnut, alive with wild birdsong;
And many a gallant homestead lay in its garden fair,
Like jewels in their setting, with blossoms often rare.

The glory of the downland that gently rose and fell
With many a patch of woodland and many a mossy dell.
No bus and little traffic moved in this quiet retreat;
The old church bells rang sweetly in its peaceful village street.

Ah me! The years fly swiftly, a change comes o'er the scene;
A different place is Banstead, the past seems like a dream.
The roads perforce were widened, the trees were all cut down,
The noisy buses came and went and we were like the town.

No longer is it country — the fairies flew away —
And trees and fields are vanishing in the Banstead of today.
Perhaps I am old-fashioned to love the country so,
But how I wish them back again, those days of long ago

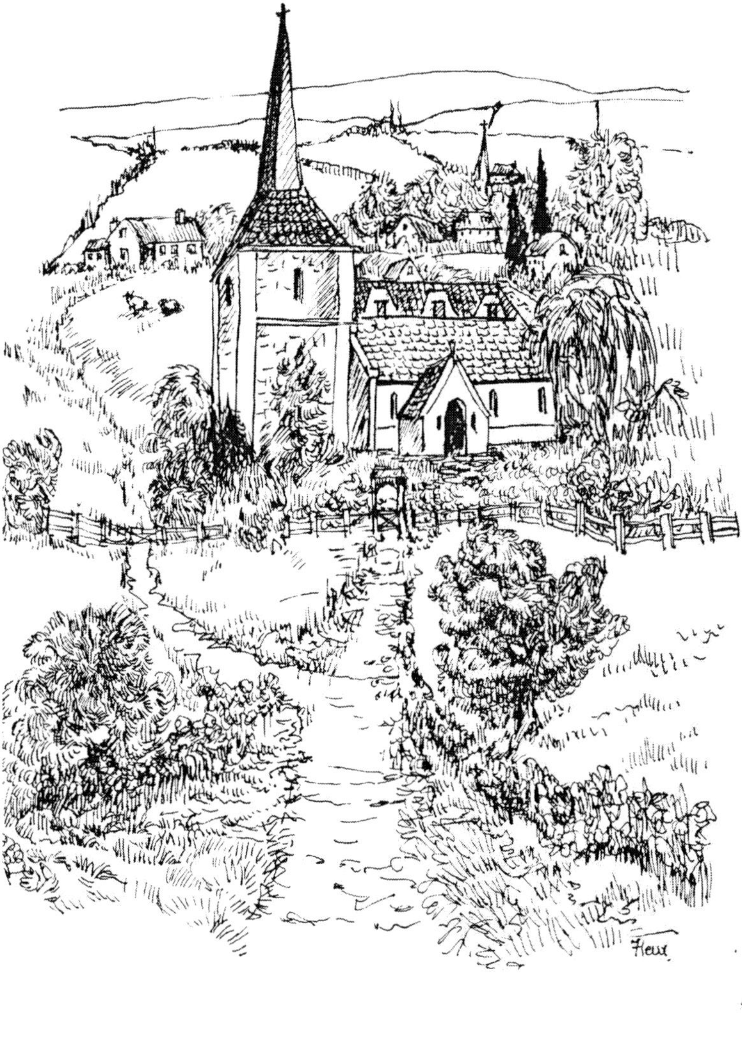
Fleur

OLD BANSTEAD

I'll sing a song of Banstead, of Banstead on the hill,
A place of downs and meadows, yet near the city's thrill;
Its little crooked village, its ancient church and steeple,
Its woods of hidden beauty, its houses and its people.

In Springtime it's a glory of green and blue and gold,
The bluebells carpet all the woods —what mystery they hold.
One thinks of gnomes and fairies a-dancing on the green,
And (let me whisper softly) real fairies have been seen.

The downland wears its mantle of lovely golden gorse,
The glory and the splendour makes one catch one's breath and pause.
And where in any village can one see more noble beeches,
The spreading branch embracing the bracken that it reaches.

And when the Summer comes around, the jaded folk from townland
Spy out our lovely country place, and picnic on the downland.
Perchance they go up higher, for those a-driving do,
And mount the hill at Reigate — Oh ! what a glorious view;
For there one gets a vista of miles of rural Surrey,
A sight for gods —or poets —a panacea for worry.

Then bye and bye comes Autumn, whose magic brush now changes
And paints the land with varying tints from brown to purple ranges,
And carpets of most gorgeous tints of green and brown and amber
Spread all along the King's highway for you and I to clamber.

And then the Winter comes —ah me ! I think I'll draw a curtain.
Of Winter joys I cannot sing, my theme here grows uncertain.
No doubt the snow, the leafless trees, all have a myriad lovers,
But gladly I would be a frog and creep to earth's warm covers.

Forgotten are the days of joy —the gladsome birdies' song,
Yes, Banstead is a lovely place, but, oh ! its winters long;
And yet I'll try to hope and smile and even try to sing,
For whilst I mope and mourn and pine —behold —
                            IT'S NEARLY SPRING !

First presented for the Ferndale Concert Party show
at the Burgh Heath Memorial Hall on Wednesday, 6th February 1929.

NONSENSE RHYMES

Oh, have you seen the Wallypug? —He's rather nice to know,
He goes abroad in sun and cloud and wallows in the snow.
He has no beard, his chin is smooth, he has a mournful cry,
His nose is snub, as you he'll rub — he has a big round eye.
"Oh why so sad, you little cad?" I asked him when we met.
He only gave a surly grunt and said "Don't be so wet;
I'm growing old, I feel the cold and it is killing me.
I must wrap up, drink cider cup and brandy in my tea.
Perhaps you'll say this sunny day that you are feeling good,
No doubt" he said "I'll soon be dead and lying in the wood."

His skin is brown — it's not quite smooth,
Indeed it's rather knobbly;
He walks not straight, perhaps you'd think
He's really somewhat wobbly.
He jumps and runs across the downs until the world grows dark,
Then hurls himself into a tree and holds on to the bark;
But not to sleep, oh no, not he — he sings a special song:
"Oh listen do, you chosen few, for I will not keep you long.
The world is gay, it's sun all day, and they have closed the pub.
So I'll buzz off - my horrid cough - my chest my wife must rub."

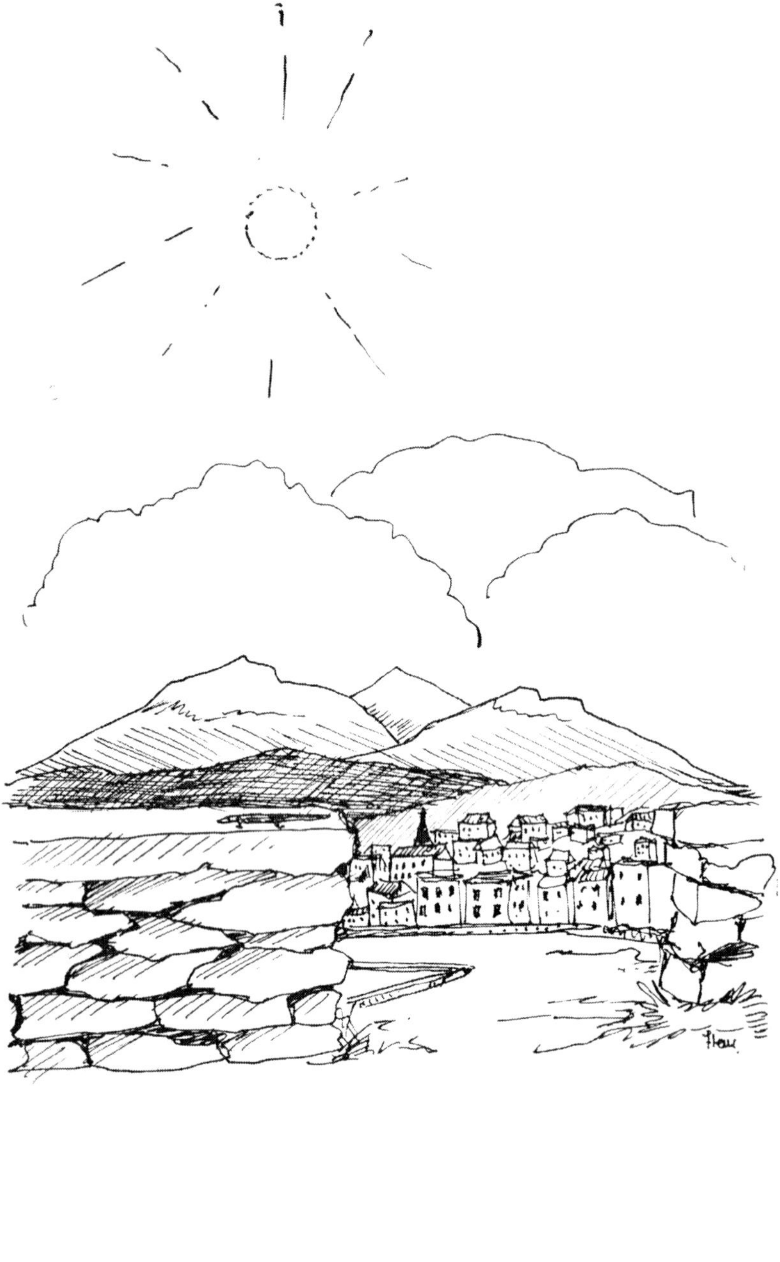

SAN SALVATORE

A lizard sat on an old stone wall
Watching the light and the shadows fall
On the ancient hills and mountains tall,
The placid lake and the waterfall
On floating cloud, and the snow-capped peak,
And the peaceful village that lay asleep
'Neath the glorious blue of the summer sky,
Watching the noise of the world pass by.

Folks came here from the city's strife
To forget the worries of business life,
To break routine, and to live in dreams
And forget the chain of mundane things,
To drink of the Lethe and forget
The woes of life that chafe and fret,
And the lizard knew in his wise old way
That the mountains would heal them all one day.

So the people came from every race
And were helped to take fresh heart of grace,
For the rugged beauty and grandeur wild
Made the hard man soft as a little child,
Whilst they seemed to catch a glimpse of His face
Who had planned the hills and fashioned the race.

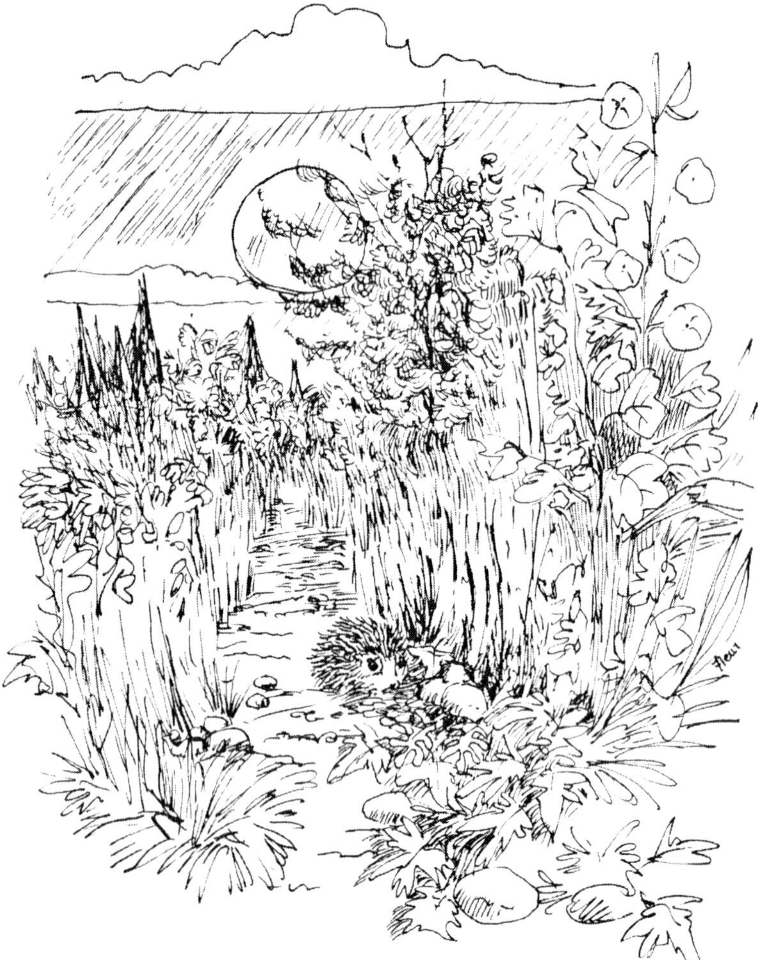

SEPTEMBER

This sweet September, oh so warm and mild,
No wind, no presage of a winter wild;
The gardens brilliant, gay with Autumn flowers,
The lessening daylight, giving rise to shorter hours.
The moon, now full, is shining on the sea
And ships sail by in silent mystery,
Their riding lights shine out in red and green
Gleaming so fairylike through moonlight sheen.
See grassy slopes backed by the dark tree hosts
Rearing tall heads like gaunt and friendly ghosts:
How beautiful, how lovely, and how still
Is sea and wood and yonder darksome hill —
How great is God showing His mighty hand
Lavishing gifts, in this our lovely land.

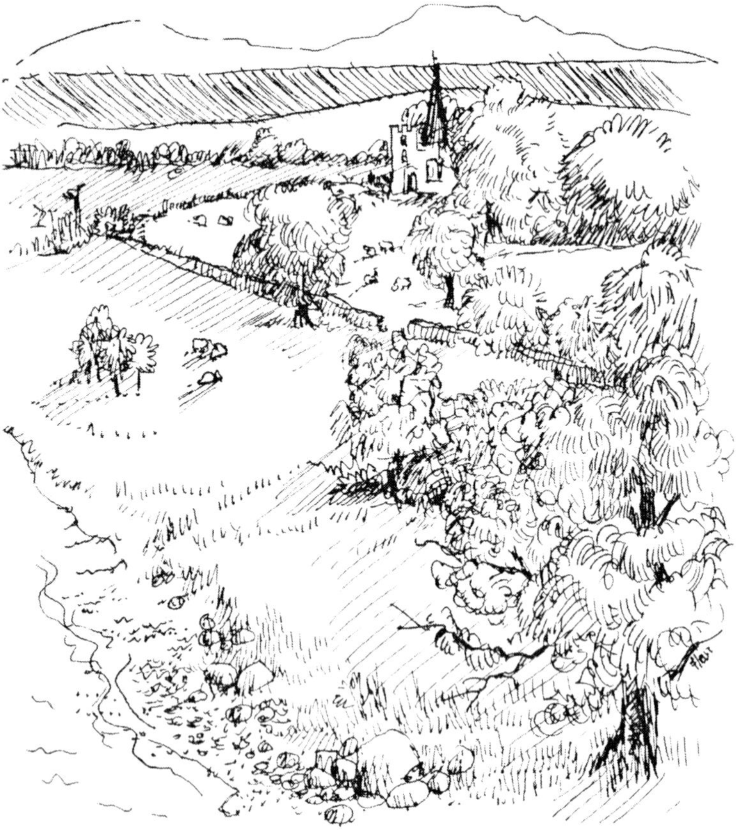

PAGHAM

I'll sing a song of Pagham — of Pagham on the beach,
A mile or two from Bognor, it isn't far to reach.
A winding lane, tree-bordered, with loudly-cawing rooks,
Beyond it cowslip meadows, with primrose-studded brooks.
Then out upon the shingle, like a long and yellow strip,
With the blue sea right and left of you, her salt upon your lip.
And to the right a blue lagoon, hedged round with gorse of gold,
Springing from stony banks framing the water cold.
Not far away, half-hidden, an ancient Church is seen,
With cattle browsing round about upon the luscious green;
And farther still are tall green trees against the noble Downs
That shut us in, and hide away the busy hive-like towns.
And when the sun shines on them they change from rose to red
And die away in purple light when late I seek my bed.

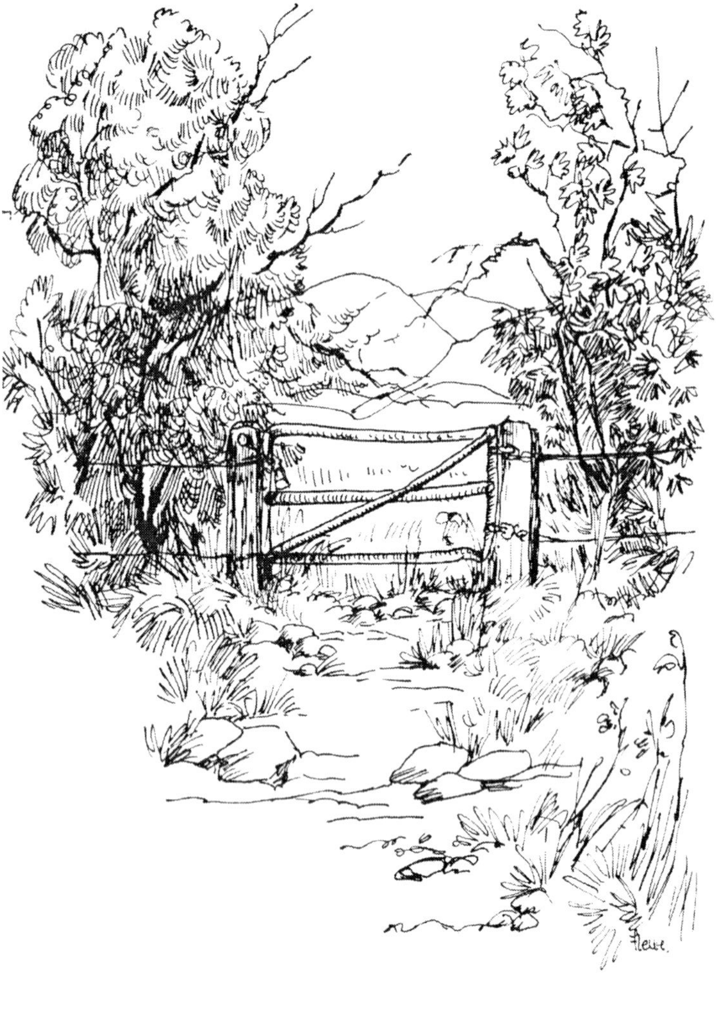

THE GATE

October's day was bright and mild:
I walked abroad and found a lane
That led to hills so steep and wild.
I wondered if they were the same
As when I was a child.

A farmyard gate now barred my way:
It was too high for me to climb.
I longed to take the path ahead;
'Twas growing dark, I'd little time.

I knew that path, its way was steep:
When I was young I'd love to go
To reach the top to get a peep
At the wide ocean down below.

The walk had tired me — I'm too old
To climb steep hills.   I turned away;
'Twas growing dark — the wind blew cold.
Maybe I'll come again another day.
Alas! Methinks it's far too late
For someone to unlatch that gate.

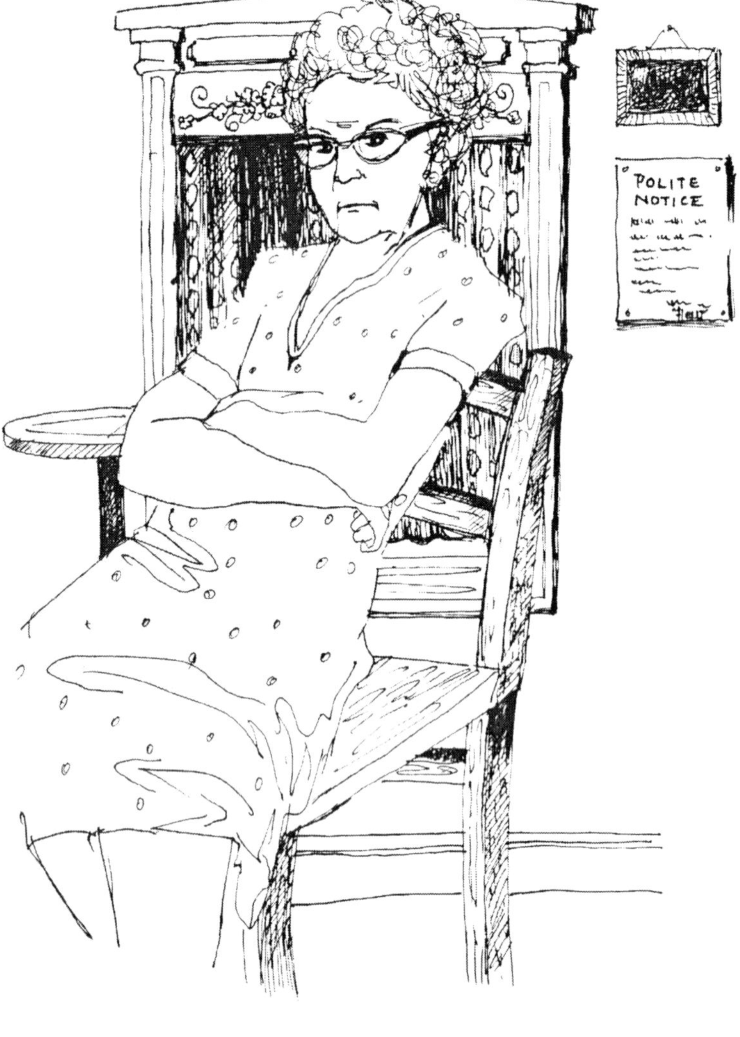
POLITE
NOTICE

WRITTEN FOR THE HARRASSED LANDLADY AT THE CARFAX

To visitors I'd like to say
I hope that you'll enjoy your stay.
I'll do my best in every way
To serve you on this holiday.
When you have gone I'll think of you
And wish you back — all but a few.
Those few, so debonair and gay,
Are lacking — this I grieve to say.
Their cigarettes, with their hot ash,
Are left about in moments rash,
And carpets, covers, tables too
Are ruined by those careless few.
The ashtray nearby is not used—
Its services are quite refused.
I wish those careless souls could be
Aware of how this vexes me:
How oft this special type of guest
Just spoils the thing for all the rest.
So to conclude, I'll thank the best
And to their conscience leave the rest.

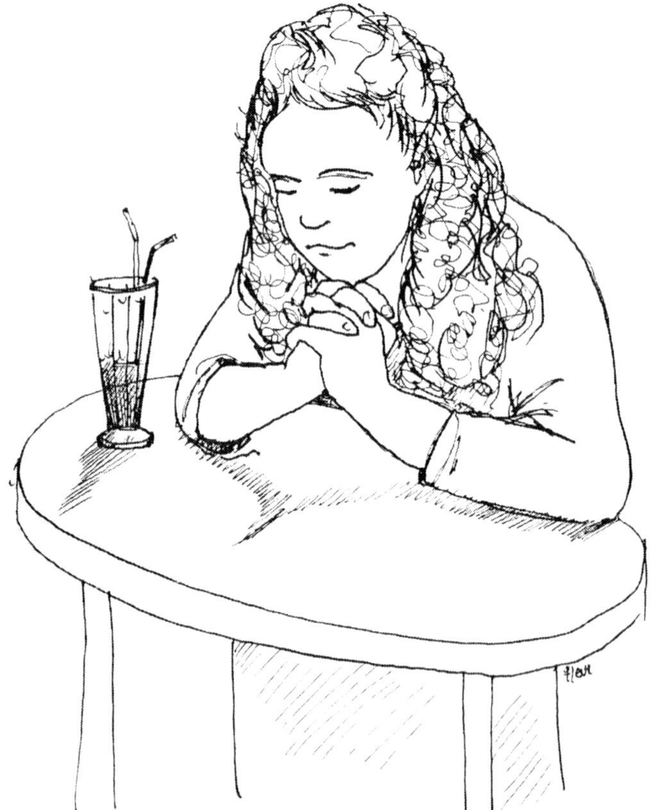

RESIGNATION

I thank Thee, Lord, for what Thou art to me;
I pray that dearer Thou wilt grow to be,
So dear that I would fain obey Thy will,
And through the strife and tumult listen still.
I want to feel the perfect trust that comes
From God Himself to all His little ones,
The trust that asks not where or what or why,
But is content in faith to live or die.
Grant me the spirit to endure each day.
Combating weakness in the finest way,
Working and striving for the general good,
Living by service as a Christian should.

A MEMORY

Written specially for Mrs. Bartram
when Flight-Lieutenant Bartram was shot down
over the North Sea

Why should I grieve for thee, O son of mine,
Though we are parted just for a time,
But through the mist I see
You still are near to me
Though veiled in mystery:
This is God's Love.

In Youth and Pride you flew the air
To drive a monster back to his lair,
Like our St. George of old,
Just such a spirit bold
Flying through heat and cold,
For love of right.

Now that your task is o'er, Knight of the Air,
Is there a single voice raised that would dare
To speak of your going in accents of pity,
Now that the gates are passed into the City
Where all true Warriors rest,
Healed there among the Blest.
For God, He knoweth best
And called you Home.

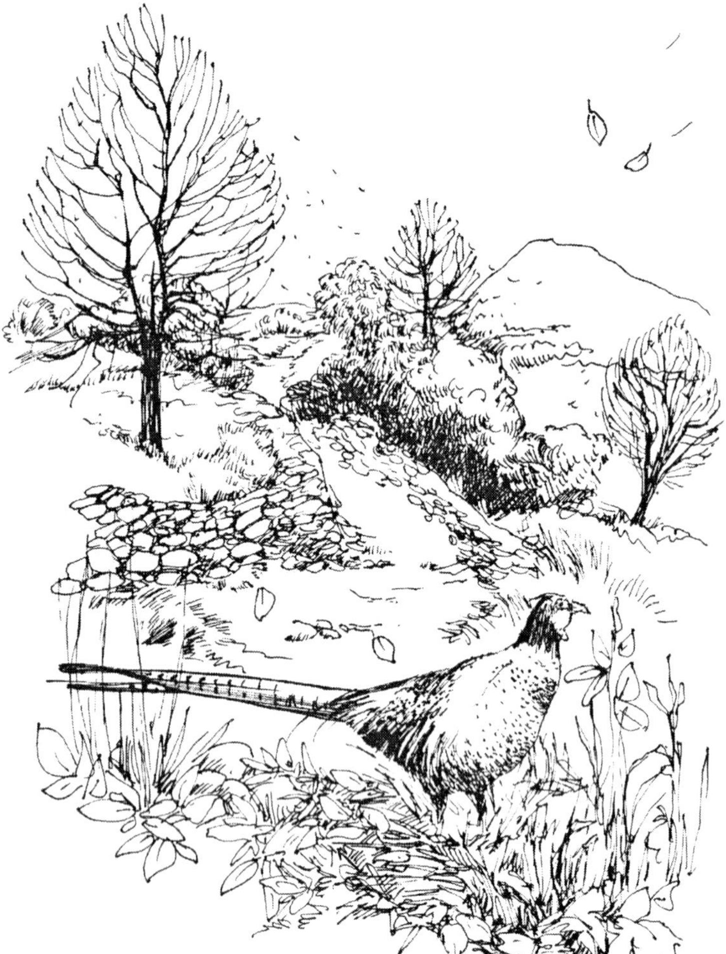
Fleur

AUTUMN AGAIN

'Tis Autumn and the hills are coldly brown;
Dead leaves, windswept, are falling swiftly down.
The tiny summer streams between the hills
Are rushing down in noisy swollen rills.
The pheasant with his raucous whirling flight
Bursts from the thicket and is lost to sight.
The hedger clips the luxury of tangle
That hid the hedges' green and graceful angle,
And ricks and barns are patched to make them warm
For cattle to lie hid from winter's storm.
The afterglows of sunset — streaks of gold —
Are dying in the West: the wind blows cold,
And breakers thunder on the rocky shore,
Telling of winter time that comes once more.
Yet every season speaks in its own way
Of life and beauty that survives decay.

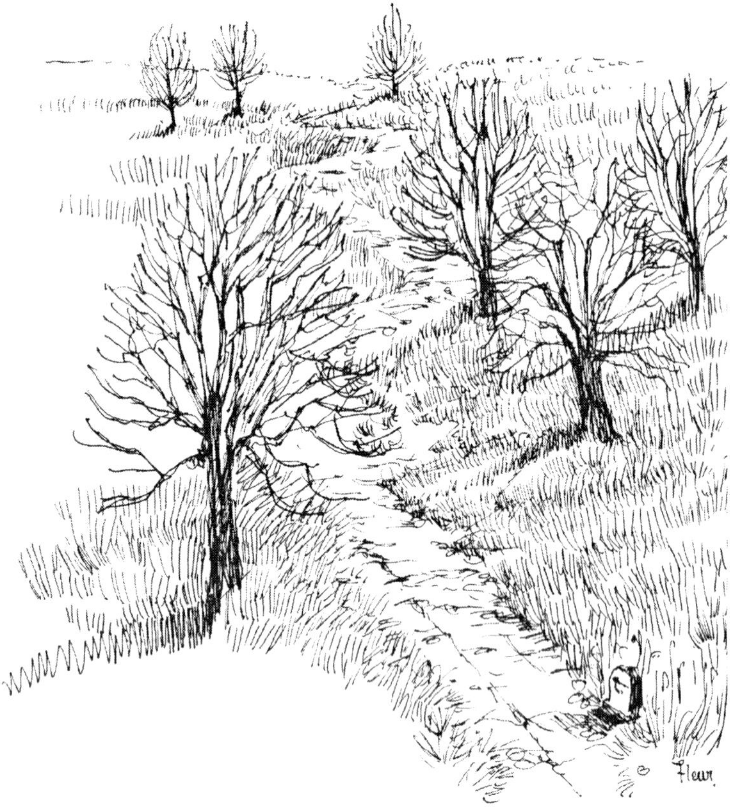

CONCLUSION

To all who are present, I wish you good health,
Much happiness and a share of wealth.
But what matters most at the close of the year —
Trust God Who alone can cast out all fear.
Our life here's a journey to conquer and fight
To shun all that's wrong and follow the right.
So now I will bid you look up and look on:
Let your life be a sermon, your living a song.
Of course you may fail and fall by the way,
But a Hand's always near to guide and to stay,
To lift and direct us, forgive us with pity,
Till we come home at last to God's heavenly city.

Cherrie's Banstead

Geoff Pushman outside the shop his mother bought in 1912

Between 1948 and 1953 Geoff Pushman, who was Cherrie's son by her first husband Mr. Edward Pushman, wrote a series of articles under the title of "Memories" for his friend Val Randall's magazine "Lights Up' (It later became 'The Banstead Spotlight'). The articles recount Geoff's early days in the Banstead area and also of the personalities who lived there at the time. The following extracts from those articles have been included here to give a flavour of the times and personalities in which Cherrie lived:

- How Cherrie Almond came to live in Banstead
- The Ferndale Concert Party of which Cherrie was a founding member writing many of the reviews and scripts.
- Willie Nash, who was a Grocer's Assistant in Cherrie's shop and who died aged 21 during the First World War.
- The Banstead War Memorial in which Cherrie was the only lady on the War Memorial Committee.

We are indebted to Mark Newell for allowing these extracts to be published alongside Geoff's Mother's poems.

The complete set of articles are available in the "Geoff's Banstead - Memories of the local area 1912 - 1948" edited by Mark Newell. You can order a copy of the book direct from the IBIS Bookshop in Banstead (109, High Street, Banstead. Tel: 01737 353260).

How Cherrie Almond came to Banstead

Early in 1912 my father, Mr. Edward Pushman, lost his job. He had been employed by the well-known firm of Charles Baker in Edgware Road. He was a tailor, and now was unable to use his right arm. At the Middlesex Hospital he was told he would have to have his arm amputated.

However, Sir Alfred Pearce Gould was put in charge of his case. He was a very well known surgeon, and he suggested a way his arm could be saved. But he would never be able to use it again as long as he lived.

Charles Baker paid him a week's wages - and that was that. There was no dole, no social security or anything like that in the world. If you had no work and no money it was the work-house. Mother was worried to death.

She would not go to her parents, and pour out her troubles. They more than likely would have said "you've made your bed -" etc. "How can I earn my living and tend a sick husband, and look after a baby", she asked herself time and time again.

The answer came from her sister Ada who lived in Wales. When she heard of mother's bleak outlook she came to her with this advice. "Take a shop - you can have them both by your side and earn your living as well". When Mother told her she knew nothing whatever about shops her sister would have no nonsense she said "you've got your brain, you'll win through".

Now mother earned in the teaching profession £45 per annum. At the end of her time she drew £60 for her final year. She had managed to save £80, but even in those days that would not buy a business. Ada promised to lend her half the balance - and talked her father (she was his favourite child) into putting up the other half. My father was against the idea. He thought they would lose the little they had.

One morning looking through the "Daily Chronicle" mother saw a shop advertised at a place called Banstead in Surrey. She had never heard of it. With grim determination she put on her outdoor

Mrs. Almond, then Mrs Pushman, with her son Geoff in 1912

clothes and took me in her arms and boarded the train to East Croydon, where the agent's office was located. There she got the address of Ferndale Stores, and the office boy was instructed to take her to West Croydon station where she would get a train to Banstead - changing at Sutton.

When she got to Sutton there was a small steam engine with a carriage back and front bound for Banstead. She looked out at the beautiful Banstead Downs on the journey and marvelled at the high cliff of chalk, and the deep chasm of chalk (no longer there) near the line as the fussy little engine steamed into Banstead Station. At the top of the stairs she enquired where Ferndale Road was and was told it was a mile further on up the Brighton Road.

Coming out of the station mother looked around. There was not a house to be seen, just the downs, and no-one in sight "How on earth can I make a shop pay here, there is not a soul to buy" she thought. It was a hot day in midsummer - a really beautiful day. She staggered up the road with me in her arms, and walked on and on up the hill.

I was a heavy baby, and, when she got to the slight bend in the road she sat on the bank and rested. The grass was green and clean in those days and the trees met overhead. It was very peaceful, and it was not much more than a lane. Not a single car or horse and cart came along. In a wood opposite there was a deep drop which she knew afterwards to be the remains of the old Roman road. It seemed so far she began to wonder if she had been misdirected.

At last a workman came along and she asked him if she was on the right road. Then she passed the Wheatsheaf - a picturesque little country pub, and found Ferndale Road - and the stores at the bottom of the road. She was a little nervous - but thankful that she had got there at last.

The owners of the shop were charming people. They took us into the sitting room and insisted we had a meal. Their name was Mr and Mrs Blakeley. They had only been there a few months. He had been a clergyman and had taken on a shop, which of course he hated. Not knowing anything about business it was lucky for mother that she had a straight man to deal with.

The shop was on a corner and was really two shops. In the larger half there was grocery, provisions, confectionary, cigarettes - and on the bend there were buckets and every sort of ironmongery hanging on hooks. It was a general shop which sold everything except coal. In the second section there was the Post Office,

The Wheatsheaf on the Brighton Road

drapery, haberdashery and a pharmacy department. The shop had been built in 1909 - (it was then 1912) and had already had two owners.

After going into the business details and looking round the shop mother was very favourably impressed with it all. Mr Blakeley employed a boy in the shop. He was about fifteen and mother took to him at once, and he agreed to stay on if she took the place. Mr Blakely got out his motorcycle and sidecar and took us back to Sutton Station. Mother took the shop. Before leaving London we paid a farewell visit to the headmistress of her old school - St Lukes Kilburn, where she had taught.

We moved to Banstead in August 1912, It was a golden summer evening, and after the furniture was arranged and mother had got things fairly straight she thought she would take a short breath of air and see what was round the corner. Wearing a summer frock she walked across the field which was fifty yards from the shop. It led into Pound Road - a narrow muddy lane with small cottages on either side, some half timbered. At the end of the road there was a clump of trees and another field with a most gorgeous view of Chipstead Valley. "I'm living in the country at last", mother thought.

The air was pure and the whole place was pervaded with a feeling of peace and beauty. Mother knew only too well that she must make a success of this business. It was a case of sink or swim. Failure would mean the poorhouse for us all. She certainly could not go again to her father for any financial help. He had already tried to prevaricate only a week before she moved. Mr Blakeley, who had already made his plans, went up to see him and after a few heated words made him see the light.

Apparently a sweet sister-in-law had made a point of coming to Banstead for a snoop round. To mothers delight she was able to go back with the information - "There are only two roads and a very prosperous shop right on the next corner - and hardly any people". Naturally enough the prospective backer got cold feet. That was how my mother became a shopkeeper.

Geoff Pushman

The Ferndale Concert Party

Mother formed a Concert Party. After much thought, she called it "The Ferndale Concert Party". Misses Bessie Wiscombe, Nona Gilbert (from the 'Victoria'), Winnie Tyrrell (John Kirby's mother), Alice Jones, Messrs Harry Green, Eddie Hobson, Bill Hobson, Mother and myself, comprised the company. We had rehearsals at our place every Tuesday night. Mother wrote a couple of one-act plays to begin with.

The Ferndale Concert Party was not the only concert party in Banstead at the time. There were 'The Racquets', a Concert Party formed at the Tennis Club. It comprised of Mr. and Mrs. Gale, Mr. and Mrs. Bromige, and a Mr.Charles Downs. Miss Orton was the pianist. They did short sketches, songs, and the usual concert party patter. Mr. Gale did a Charlie Chaplin kind of role in the comedy sketches. Mr. Downs was the broad comedian, and Mrs. Bromige had the singing voice.

'To get them to sing' has always been a great problem. None of our girls could sing, and Harry Green, in charge of the musical side, used to coax and even get mildly sarcastic all to no avail.

We only had one singer in the Troupe, and that was Bill Hobson, who had a fine voice. Mother and I could sing, so the whole chorus work almost rested on our shoulders, for apart from Alice Jones, the girls had no voices at all, and were only too ready to admit it. What we lacked in vocal roles, we made up for in the acting line. Eddie Hobson was an excellent light comedian, and Bessie Wiscombe, Winnie Tyrrell and Nora Gilbert were all extraordinarily good actresses.

We did a show at the Institute and raised money to build the gate at the side, for the only entrance was up the steps. There was no way up for prams or bikes till then. Then we did the same show at Burgh Heath for the Middlesex Hospital.

'The Ferndale Concert Party' met at our house every Tuesday night, from the end of August till the beginning of January to rehearse for the concert to be given in January. All the members of the company were in their teens, and were full of high spirits and full of fun. They were mostly in the Tennis Club, and all went dancing together.

Mother produced the show, and looking back, I think it was a very good show. Maybe it was that they were all friendly together accounted for the excellent team work — they were the youth of the day. There was plenty of hard work done for Mother kept them at it also plenty of the lighter side. For instance, when Bill Hobson forgot his lines at rehearsal and kept saying to extemporise "This is alright, this is" when supposed to be pleased.

Harry Green's bright little remarks such as "Take him to the block" when a prospective country cousin in a play is to be taken to see the Tower of London.

We opened at the Institute, the show being in aid of building a new gate there. Now Bill Hobson was to sing a duet with a lady—a comedy song. There was not a lady in the company with a strong enough voice to stand up to him. There was a lot of humming and hahing and they could not come to any decision. Then I stepped forward and asked to take it. I had never done a female impersonation in my life, but felt I could. I had bought a wig from a boy at school, a blonde one, for 8d., so was partly prepared.

Mother could not imagine me doing it as I had anything but a feminine face. Harry Green and Bill Hobson favoured the idea. I could wear the wig, mother's size four shoes, and I had a high voice I was only just fourteen. I got the chance. What difficulties we had in those days !

The Institute had no stage, so half-a-dozen billiard tables were erected together for shows. We of course used the billiard tables that meant no stage lighting. So mother begged, borrowed, or acquired, as many acetylene lamps she could. She then made cardboard shields nailed to wooden slats, which were nailed to the edge of the tables. We had screens for a background which mother decorated with bright crepe paper and material. Just before the show, to check up on the acetylene lamps, Tom Gilbert volunteered to see they were full of carbide and working well. His sister, Nona, was in the troupe.

Then, as the show opened, the lamps dimmed and began to splutter. They of course worked perfectly before we began. A fine opening just when you want all you can get to help you along. So

The Ferndale Concert Party(1928)
Cherrie seated, first from the left. Geoff is standing in the centre at the back.

The Ferndale Concert Party(1928)
Cherrie, third from the left with Geoff second from the right.

mother appealed to any member of the audience who understood acetylene lamps to lend a hand. Mr. Poole came forward and did the trick, In spite of a poor start (which was a misfortune and not very helpful to us) we got going.

Bill Hobson sang 'My Prayer' and another ballad. Mother recited 'Little orphan Annie'. Eddie Hobson did a droll comedy number called 'The Rabbit'. Alice Jones sang 'Pasadena' and 'What'll I Do'. Bill Hobson and I did our duet. I had recently seen (or heard) Miss Carrie Tubb, the singer, at Bournemouth. So I was supposed to be a haughty type of dame. I called myself Miss Tarrie Cubb on the programme. It went over big the more Bill became familiar and dashing with me, the more scornful and fierce I became. The audience yelled. Then Bill got more dashing than ever and out went his arm and he gave the screen a mighty punch. Over went the screen bang on me, and there was I buried under it ! I believe the audience thought it was all part of the show. Our act together was a wow and set me thinking up other female impersonations I would give.

Mother wrote 'Finding Robert' in which Bessie Wiscombe gave such a good comedy character performance. Winnie Tyrrell, Harry Green, Bill Hobson, Alice Jones and Eddie Hobson also did wonderfully well, the audience rocked with laughter at them, and it couldn't have been done better. I sang 'Mister Waterhouse's House.' To conclude, we presented a straight sketch which Mother wrote lasting 30 minutes called 'Play The Game' — with the whole company. I had the part of a school-boy with a passion for cricket, and I clutched a cricket bat in quite a bit of the play. I had to recite that very fine poem 'Play The Game' in the play. It was my first straight turn, and I was naturally anxious, but it was alright.

We were dressed in Pierrot costume for the concerted item, but in character for the plays. Anyway, the show was very well received and we were all very thrilled. Bill Hobson with his usual good nature was very upset because Mother hadn't mentioned on the programme that she had written the plays. So after 'The King' he dashed up on the stage to tell the audience so. But he got up there before he had made up his mind what to say. He called for silence, and then he realised he was there, and all he said was "It's jolly good —— it's a good show." The audience did not know quite what he was getting at, but clapped harder than ever.

Programme

FERNDALE CONCERT PARTY
Wednesday, 6th February, 1929.

THE FAMOUS WALTZ	... ...	THE COMPANY
OPENING CHORUS	... ...	THE COMPANY
SONG	... "Leanin" ...	Geoffrey Pushman
SONG	... "Two's Company, Threes None" ...	Hetty Brooker
RECITATION	... ...	Mrs. Pushman

"The Belles and the Bootblacks" ... ...
 Leonard Cave, Arthur Brooker, Winnie Burgess and Hetty Brooker.

SONG ... ... THE COMPANY

"SHOPPING"—
Arthur Brooker, Vera Privett, Winnie Burgess and Geoffrey Pushman.

INTERVAL.

CONCERTED ITEM	.. "Fancy v. Fact" ...	THE COMPANY
SONG	... ...	Mr. CUTTS
"A SEASIDE ROMANCE"	...	Enid Willmott and Jack Brant
COMIC SONG	... ...	Geoffrey Pushman
DUET	... "I've Got Something to Say to You"	... ...

Vera Privett and Geoffrey Pushman.

"THUMBS UP"	... ...	THE COMPANY
"THE MOUTE BANK WALTZ"	... ...	THE COMPANY
"INDIA"	Eastern Episode	... ...

Jack Brant, Geoffrey Pushman and Leonard Cave.

SKETCH—
"When is a Niece not a Niece" or "The Nice Niece"
THE COMPANY.

"BEDTIME" ... ... THE COMPANY

GOD SAVE THE KING.

The programme for the concert held on 6th February 1928 by the Ferndale Concert Party.

How thrilled we all were the next week at Burgh Heath War Memorial Hall when a telegram arrived from the Middlesex Hospital just before the curtain went up wishing us the best of luck for our show. Having a real stage there, it made everything plain sailing. At the conclusion of the show, a bouquet was handed up to Mother from the Company, and a box of chocolates with a card attached which read "To Miss Tarrie Cubb from a well-wisher." I was thrilled to bits and very happy. I have the card to this day. I found out some time later the chocolates were from Mrs. Green who, with her usual thought and kindliness, knew it would give me pleasure.

One reason for the splendid team-work of that Company was no doubt because Eddie and Bill Hobson and Harry Green were all cousins (Bill is brother to our Mr. Hobson). Later Nona Gilbert married Harry Green who became a cleric, and to add to that, Bessie Wiscombe and Winnie Tyrrell married two brothers ! Anyway, in the final scene of 'Play The Game' they were all paired off with each other — except Winnie Tyrrell who had to make do with me, saying "that has promised to wait till I grow up." What happened after rehearsal I was too young to know. No doubt the boys saw the girls home, for often a long time afterwards when out with the dog I'd come across one of the boys walking home alone.

The Ferndale Concert Party is reborn
Owing to my Father's long illness, and death, we were unable to do any stage shows for a long time afterwards. Anyway, in September 1928 we began to reform The Ferndale Concert Party. All the old members had drifted, some had married, some had other interests, so we began to collect an entirely new cast. We got two old friends of mine, Arthur Brooker and his sister Eileen (whom we called Hetty) Jack Brant, Enid Willmott and Winnie Burgess. I was very anxious for another old friend of mine, Len Cave, to try his hand at acting, but he was very shy and did not relish the idea at all.

Anyway, on the night of the first rehearsal, at our place, I came across Len at his gate doing nothing and asked him if he wouldn't come along and just take the piano and act as accompanist for rehearsals. He came. Then the crowd began to arrive for the first rehearsal. Enid Willmott brought along two girl friends of hers, Vera Privett and Joyce Goldfinch, and we began work. Miss Goldfinch never came again, but all the others were very enthusiastic and eager to do all they could to make the show a success. Leonard Cave got roped in for a large part of course and did very well indeed.

All this company was round about my own age, they were my contemporaries. It was a very strong company and, what was a great advantage, nearly all of them could sing. There was next to no social life in Banstead in those days, youth clubs were unheard of, so it was an event to come to rehearsal, and we all got a great kick out of it.

Although we had plenty of fun we worked hard, and achieved a well rehearsed, polished little show. We-had no hall to rehearse in, no band at the show, no scenery or elaborate costumes. All our rehearsing was done in the room behind the shop next door to where I live now.

Hetty Brooker had a lovely voice and put over a song very well. She was really more of a concert artiste than an actress. Vera Privett had a grand sense of comedy, although she had a good voice, she was more of an actress. Enid Willmott was very good indeed in character roles and was a grand actress. Len Cave displayed a keen sense of humour and was a good all round player. Jack Brant and Arthur Brooker were also very good, and Winnie Burgess did very well indeed.

As I said before, it was a good company. Mother kept them working hard at it, and they all pulled their weight. On the night of the show, Wednesday, 6th February 1929, mother had spent all the afternoon decorating the back of the stage with crepe paper. It made a most elaborate background and took away that bare, drab back of stage look.

Going up to Burgh Heath, it was a thrill to see the crowds queuing for the bus, and to hear them call out greetings and good wishes for the success of the show. As we were getting dressed, a telegram arrived from the Middlesex Hospital for which we were giving the show wishing us luck. Miss Florrie Whittington was our accompanist at the piano.

We had a very attractive concerted number called 'The Famous Mountebank Waltz' and we introduced it before we plunged into the opening chorus. My voice had broken by this time and I sang my very first serious song 'Leanin'. Then Hetty Brooker sang 'Two's Company, Three's None,' — the evening was already going well.

Mother had written a poem entitled 'Banstead' (which you will find in this book). She wrote it specially for this show, and it went over very well. It is, I think, one of the best she has ever written, and it was a novelty to hear her recite her own composition.

Leonard Cave, Arthur Brooker, Winnie Burgess and Hetty Brooker did a very appealing number called 'The Belles and the Bootblacks,' and Arthur Brooker, Vera Privett, Winnie Burgess and myself did a comedy sketch entitled 'Shopping.'

There were a couple of concerted items 'Song of the Sea' which we all sang lustily, and 'Thumbs Up,' and we had a reprisal of 'The Famous Waltz'. Enid Willmott and Jack Brant did a comedy scene 'A Seaside Romance'

I sang two comedy songs 'I Can't Make Green Peas Stop On My Knife' and 'I'm Going to Take a Water Melon to my Girl Tonight.' I then partnered Vera Privett in a duet 'I've got Something to Say to You,' and I found in Miss Privett a marvellous partner. She was calm and richly humorous and was a perfect foil for my energetic antics. We went over well together.

'India' was a very amusing comic caper with Jack Brant, Len Cave and myself, with our faces covered with cocoa and wearing native costume, while Hetty Brooker did an oriental dance as Kirlibaba.

To rest the company, we had a turn by a visiting artiste. Mr. Cutts had promised to give us a song, but at the very last minute he was unable to appear. So, rather than let us down, Mrs. Cutts, out of the kindness of her heart, deputised for him and sang 'Wait' and 'Smilin' Through.' She had not rehearsed at all, but just came along and did a good job.

To conclude the evening the usual sketch. It was in two acts and lasted over half an hour 'When is a Niece not a Niece ?' or 'The Nice Niece' with the entire Company. It was a sort of 'Charley's Aunt' affair with me doing a female impersonation. Enid Willmott did very well as a comic maid, and Len Cave as an amorous suitor. Mother wrote the play.

Admission was only sixpence and a shilling, and we raised £10 for the Middlesex Hospital. That gives you an idea of the sort of shows we used to have here in 1929. We saw to our own costumes, and apart from character sketches we wore pierrot clothes. As you can guess by the results, the hall was crowded. I saw several of my

Nork customers there and of course all the locals. I don't know who enjoyed themselves most, the audience or the performers.

It was grand to see Mrs. Butler (who never missed any of our shows) and Mrs. Killick, and all the familiar faces in the crowded audience. We had to repeat the show at the Banstead Institute. They had just built the stage there and the new Men's Club. The acoustics were terrible, the sound got lost in the top of the stage, but we managed to get it over somehow. Afterwards they filled in the ceiling over the stage and made it sound-worthy.

Geoff Pushman

Willie Nash

Mother had always been passionately fond of the country, and she found it difficult to believe she was really living in the country at last. She hated Kilburn. On that first night, after she had got a bit straight, she thought she must know what lay beyond the field. It was a lovely night, and she walked, hatless and alone, towards the Pound, and turned towards what was then Edgelers shop. She looked down the "stoney road" and thought what a lovely view it was and what a marvellous place actually to live in. The air was so pure, and everything so beautiful.

We had a young man working for us in the shop called Willie Nash. I was very fond of Willie, took to him at once, and he was very fond of me. He used to spoil me. Most fellows of his age would not want to be seen with children, but it was no uncommon thing for him to push me up the road in my pushchair.

He used to be weighing up the sugar and singing all the songs of the day, and of course taught me all the words of the songs. I used to love to see him weigh up "yellow crystals" (a cheap brown sugar). The white had no attraction for me. "Weigh up 'yellow crystals' this afternoon, Willie," I used to say, "and we'll sing".

William John Nash (1897-1918)

Now Grandma up in London had a gramophone with a huge red horn. I used to spend hours playing it and listening to it. —Florrie Forde singing "Come In The Parlour Charlie", "Mary's Ticket", "Do Drop In At the Dew-Drop Inn"; a chap singing, "My Wife's Gone To The Country"; but best of all I liked Billy Williams singing; "When Father Papered The Parlour",. I knew them all by heart, backwards, and of course sang them through for Willie.

One day Willie came to work with great excitement. He had bought a gramophone and would I come round to his house and see it. There it was in the front room—red horn and all (just like the one Grandma had), and, joy upon joy, the record of Billy Williams singing "When Father Papered The Parlour". How thrilled we both were!

Billy Williams created at great impression on my early life. To me he was a real comic. The Man In The Velvet Suit they called him. He would have made his fortune on the wireless —such a clear cheery voice, and his diction was perfect.

Willie Nash was my first friend and partner in the singing of comic songs. Two of our 'speciality numbers' I remember were "Hold Your Hand Out, Naughty Boy" and "Hullo, Hullo, Who's Your Lady Friend?"

The War broke out in 1914. The Germans had marched into Belgium. Willie was one of the first to volunteer. (He put his age on a year, being only seventeen). I remember he stood up against the door and we scratched his height on it to see if he had grown next time we saw him. He never came back.

Geoff Pushman

Private William John Nash
31863, 12/13th Bn., Northumberland Fusiliers

Willie Nash was killed in action in Aisne, France on May 27 1918 aged 21. At the time he was with the Northumberland Fusiliers. In August 1914, the original British Expeditionary Force crossed the Aisne in August 1914 a few kilometres west of Soissons, and re-crossed it in September a few kilometres east. For the next three and half years, this part of the front was held by French forces and the city remained within range of German artillery. At the end of April 1918, five divisions of Commonwealth forces (IX Corps) were posted to the French 6th Army in this sector to rest and refit following German offensives on the Somme and Lys. Here, at the

Soissons Memorial, Aisne, France

World War I memorial in Banstead Church yard (2006)

end of May, they found themselves facing the overwhelming German attack which, despite fierce opposition, pushed the Allies back across the Aisne to the Marne.

Willie Nash's name together with almost 4,000 officers and men of the United Kingdom forces who died during the battles of the Aisne and Marne in 1918 and who have no known grave are commemorated on the Soissons Memorial.

His name is also commemorated on the Banstead War Memorial and on the World War I memorial in Banstead churchyard.

The Banstead War Memorial

Where the War Memorial stands now there used to be a clump of laurel bushes caged in an iron fence. It was decided to build a Memorial, and a collection was made from the whole village. My Mother was the only lady on the War Memorial Committee which consisted, besides herself, of Mr. Gale, Mr. Bob Webb, Sir Henry Lambert, Sir Ralph Neville, Mr. Maynard Taylor, and the Vicar.

Mr. Maynard Taylor advocated a horse trough, but Mother reminded him that in ten years from then there would be no horses on the road—something which they could not believe. She was, of course, right. Horse traffic faded from the roads during that time.

Mother tried hard for a hall to be built on Horsecroft (Shallcross's field), but the land was too expensive. She thought a hall would have been the thing the men who had given their lives would have wanted themselves. However, a monument was decided upon, and Mother therefore advocated that it should be erected at the end of Garratts Lane—half way between the two areas. She was outnumbered, and the War Memorial was built where it is now.

We were a community of our own —not joined on to the village by buildings as we are today. We were not Burgh Heath and not fully Banstead. Whenever anyone passed a disparaging remark about us Mother reminded them that we were, after all, the West end and civilization always spreads Westwards !

The War Memorial, Banstead (2006)